ANTWERP
THE CITY AT A GLAN

Antwerp Tower
Built in 1974 and now undergoin
renovation, the 87m Antwerp To
tallest building in the Diamond D
De Keyserlei 5

Centraal Station
One of architect Louis Delacenserie's most
representative works, this is one of the finest
examples of eclecticism in Belgium, and is
often referred to as the Railway Cathedral.
Koningin Astridplein 27

Cathedral of Our Lady
The Onze-Lieve-Vrouwekathedraal was built
in 1521 and remains one of Antwerp's most
prominent landmarks, distinctive for having
only one, fully complete, 123m-high tower.
See p011

KBC Tower
This art deco-style high-rise, finished in 1932,
was the first steel-framed structure in Belgium.
See p015

Bourla Theatre
Named after its architect, Pierre Bruno
Bourla, this theatre hosts plays, concerts
and dance in an 1834 neoclassical building.
Komedieplaats 18, T 03 224 8844

Oudaan Police Tower
Completed in 1967, the Police Tower was
designed by Renaat Braem, one of Belgium's
most celebrated modernist architects.
See p010

Sint-Annatunnel
Connecting the Old City with Linkeroever,
this pedestrian tunnel features beautiful twin
art deco entrances, one on each riverbank.
See p014

INTRODUCTION

THE CHANGING FACE OF THE URBAN SCENE

Few cities have balanced culture and commerce as successfully as Antwerp. Strategically located on the Scheldt, a breath away from France, the Netherlands and Germany, this north Belgian city and capital of the Dutch-speaking province of Flanders has been the home of seminal artists, such as the baroque painters Peter Paul Rubens and Anthony Van Dyck, one of Europe's most important merchant ports, and the centre of the world's diamond trade. More recently, the emergence in the 1980s of the Antwerp Six, including the influential designers Dirk Bikkembergs, Ann Demeulemeester, Walter Van Beirendonck and Dries Van Noten, propelled the city to the fashion industry's cutting edge and led to the creation of institutions such as ModeNatie (see p029).

In the past few decades, there have been no signs of a slowdown in Antwerp's creative energy. The redevelopment of the dockland area, Het Eilandje, has carved out a new urban hot zone, boasting hip bars and eateries, residential complexes and museums, while the established districts of Meir and trendsetting Zuid keep both visitors and locals buoyant with edgy boutiques, Michelin-starred restaurants, galleries and clubs. Add to the mix Antwerp's architectural highlights, from its 16th-century guildhouses to the art nouveau treasures of Zurenborg and modernist classics such as Renaat Braem's Police Tower (see p010), and you'll see there are myriad gems to be discovered in this small but fascinating city.

ESSENTIAL INFO
FACTS, FIGURES AND USEFUL ADDRESSES

TOURIST OFFICE
Grote Markt 13
T 03 232 0103
antwerpen.be

TRANSPORT
Car hire
Hertz
T 03 239 2921
hertz.com
Metro/Rail/Tram
Große Handstraat 58
T 03 218 1411
delijn.be
Taxis
Antwerp Taxi
Karel Oomsstraat 14
T 03 238 3838

EMERGENCY SERVICES
Ambulance
T 100
Fire
T 100
Police
T 101
Police information
T 0800 12 312
Late-night pharmacy
T 1207

EMBASSIES
British Embassy
85 rue d'Arlon
Brussels
T 02 287 6211
www.britishembassy.gov.uk/belgium
US Embassy
27 boulevard du Régent
Brussels
T 02 508 2111
belgium.usembassy.gov

MONEY
American Express
T 02 676 2121
travel.americanexpress.com

POSTAL SERVICES
Post Office
Pelikaanstraat 16
T 03 229 0380
Shipping
DHL
Merantistraat 1
T 02 715 5050
www.dhl.be

BOOKS
Antwerp by Nicholas Royle (Serpent's Tail)
Good Beer Guide to Belgium by Tim Webb (CAMRA Books)
Lofts of Antwerp by Bert Verbeke (Exhibitions International)

WEBSITES
Architecture
www.vai.be
Fashion
modenatie.com
Newspaper
www.gva.be

COST OF LIVING
Taxi from Antwerp Airport to city centre
£15
Cappuccino
£2.25
Packet of cigarettes
£3.75
Daily newspaper
£0.75
Bottle of champagne
£45

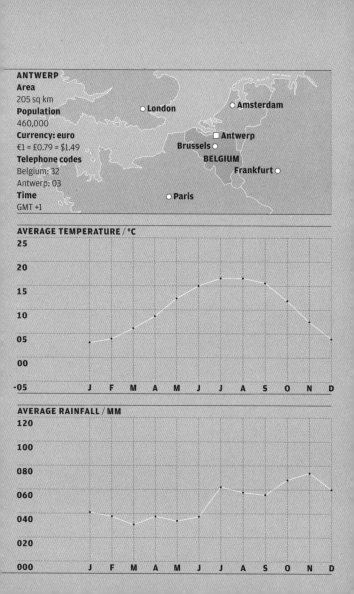

ANTWERP
Area
205 sq km
Population
460,000
Currency: euro
€1 = £0.79 = $1.49
Telephone codes
Belgium: 32
Antwerp: 03
Time
GMT +1

London   Amsterdam
Antwerp
Brussels
BELGIUM
Frankfurt
Paris

AVERAGE TEMPERATURE / °C

	J	F	M	A	M	J	J	A	S	O	N	D

25
20
15
10
05
00
-05

AVERAGE RAINFALL / MM

120
100
080
060
040
020
000

| J | F | M | A | M | J | J | A | S | O | N | D |

NEIGHBOURHOODS

THE AREAS YOU NEED TO KNOW AND WHY

To help you navigate the city, we've chosen the most interesting districts (see below and the map inside the back cover) and colour-coded our featured venues, according to their location; those venues that are outside these areas are not coloured.

HET EILANDJE

The city's port since the 16th century, the old dock has now been dredged and its warehouses transformed into upmarket clubs and restaurants. A number of luxury residential projects are underway, while the Sint-Felix Pakhuis (see p070) and the maritime-focused Museum Aan de Stroom (mas.be), due to open in 2010, confirm the area's arrival on the city's cultural map. The adjacent Old Merchant Quarter is home to the university and the red-light district.

OLD CITY

The majority of Antwerp's monuments and historical attractions are concentrated here, including the cathedral (see p011), the Brabo fountain, the Town Hall and Butcher's Hall. Quirky shops and the former home of Flemish baroque painter Jacob Jordaens (Reyndersstraat 6) are tucked among the narrow, cobblestoned streets, centuries-old townhouses, gabled guildhouses and charming squares.

MEIR

The city's main shopping district, the Meir boasts both high-street stores and designer boutiques. Here you'll also find the HQs of several banking and insurance companies, as well as plenty of enticing waffle shops. Home to the aristocracy in the 17th and 18th centuries, which is evident in the area's rococo architecture, the Meir is also the location of Peter Paul Rubens' house (see p024), now a museum.

ZURENBORG

Despite being cut in half by railway tracks, Zurenborg's pleasant squares, Draakplaats and Dageraadplaats, its villagey vibe and impressive architecture make it one of the city's most beautiful zones. Its art nouveau and art deco houses, the most striking of which are on Cogels-Osylei, are populated by artists and intellectuals. The old tram company offices, and the excellent Dôme and Dôme sur Mer (see p040) restaurants are also to be found in Zurenborg.

SINT-ANDRIES AND ZUID

These happening 'hoods are all about cool eateries, contemporary art galleries, museums, fashion and antiques. Here are the flagship stores for Walter (see p080) and Dries Van Noten (see p082) among others, and Koosterstraat, the heart of the city's burgeoning antiques market. The south end of Nationalestraat is Zuid's hub. Richard Rogers' Law Courts (see p012) lie at the tip of the area on Bolivarplaats.

DIAMOND DISTRICT

The city's first diamond traders settled here in the 16th century, and today, this densely packed area still bristles with merchants' offices and jewellers. To find out more about the world's pre-eminent diamond centre, visit the Diamantmuseum (Koningin Astridplein 19-23, T 03 202 4890), located on the same square as Centraal Station (see p009), which features permanent and temporary exhibitions.

LANDMARKS

THE SHAPE OF THE CITY SKYLINE

Despite its architectural diversity, Antwerp has always remained relatively low-level – the centre's townhouses rarely exceed four storeys and the city's big, modernist residential blocks have been confined to the suburbs. Up until now, just three buildings have dominated the skyline, at least in terms of their height: the Oudaan Police Tower (see p010), KBC Tower (see p015) and the imposing spire of the Cathedral of Our Lady (see p011). Yet the cityscape is transforming. Six high-rises, two designed by David Chipperfield, are slated to be built from 2009 as part of the ongoing development of Het Eilandje, giving the city some new, northerly focal points.

The best views of Antwerp's existing landmarks are from the west bank of the Scheldt, which you visit via the wonderful twin 1930s entrance buildings of the underground pedestrian Sint-Annatunnel (see p014), which crosses from one side of the river to the other. And not to be missed is the Centraal Station (Koningin Astridplein 27), whose heavily decorated façade and metal-and-glass dome overshadow the surrounding streets. Dubbed the 'Railway Cathedral', its extended train shed and tracks cut through the Diamond District and define Zurenborg's limits. To the south-east, in Zuid, the Royal Museum of Fine Arts, or KMSKA (Leopold De Waelplaats, T 03 238 7809), sits like an ancient temple on top of a monumental staircase, and is the area's point of reference. *For full addresses, see Resources.*

Oudaan Police Tower

Designed by one of Belgium's finest modernists, Renaat Braem, working in collaboration with Juul De Roover and Maxime Wijnants, Oudaan Police Tower looms over the fashionable Kleine Markt square. The original plan was for two towers connected by a lower building, and an entire city block was demolished in the 1950s to make way for the construction. However, only one tower was completed, in 1967, and this now houses Antwerp's police HQ. The public can access the 12th floor, where the Metropolitan Police Museum is located (visits by appointment only) and the city views are impressive. Braem's somewhat brutalist design, which features a few Gothic-like flourishes on the façade – the sculptured lines between the windows – still divides local opinion.

Oudaan 5, T 03 202 5828

Cathedral of Our Lady

As in many historic European cities, the cathedral dominates the centre. Antwerp's Cathedral of Our Lady (also known as Onze-Lieve-Vrouwekathedraal) took 169 years to build and, when finished in 1521, it became the largest Gothic construction in the Low Countries, despite only one of the two planned 123m spires having been completed. In addition to the gloriously detailed stonework and sculpture, period craftwork and 55 stained-glass windows that illuminate its seven high bays, the cathedral boasts original paintings by Rubens. Following extensive renovations spanning nearly 30 years, Our Lady was designated a World Heritage Site in 1999 and is considered one of Europe's most architecturally important cathedrals. *Handschoenmarkt, T 03 213 9951, www.dekathedraal.be*

Law Courts

Opened in 2006, Antwerp's Law Courts, designed by Richard Rogers Partnership (now Rogers Stirk Harbour + Partners) and locally based architects Bureau Van Kerckhove, stands out on Antwerp's southern skyline. Although it's a low structure, the dramatic sail-like roofline is visible from the edge of the city centre. Each roof 'pod', formed from a steelwork frame and interconnected concrete units, houses a courtroom, while the rest of the building incorporates hearing rooms, offices, archive space and a central public hall. Extended glazing maximises the natural light and ventilation, reinforcing the sense of transparency and accessibility. *Bolivarplaats 20, T 03 257 8011*

Sint-Annatunnel

Most of Antwerp is located on the east bank of the Scheldt, though the residential west bank (Linkeroever) is still worth a trip, if only to enjoy the views of the city and port in a quieter setting. The best way to cross the river is to walk underneath it, via the Sint-Annatunnel. Each entrance is marked by a handsome art deco building (above), whose original 1930s lifts and wooden escalators are still in operation,

to take pedestrians down to the 572m, white-tiled tunnel. After a 10-minute stroll, you'll emerge on the west bank in the middle of a small park.

Sint-Jansvliet and Frederik van Eedenplein

KBC Tower

This tower, built to house apartments and the KBC bank, was constructed on a WWI bomb site in the run-up to the 1930 World Exhibition held in Antwerp. Often cited as Europe's first skyscraper, it was completed in 1932 and soon nicknamed Boerentoren (Farmers' Tower), as the bank's major shareholder at the time was a farmers' association. Its architect, Jan van Hoenacker, designed a 87.5m-tall structure, and the first in the country to incorporate a steel frame, though the height was increased to 97m in 1976. Its reinforced concrete-plate foundations and 34,000 tons of steel helped the building to survive the WWII bombings that destroyed so much of the city, and in 1981 it was declared a National Protected Monument, thus securing its future.
Schoenmarkt 35

HOTELS

WHERE TO STAY AND WHICH ROOMS TO BOOK

For such a small city, Antwerp has a wealth of fine places to stay to suit all tastes and budgets. Most of the big-name chains are here, including Radisson and Scandic, a Michael Graves-designed Astrid Park Plaza (Koningin Astridplein 7, T 03 203 1234) and a baroque-style Hilton (Groenplaats, T 03 204 1212), but it's the city's charming B&Bs that steal the show. Located throughout Antwerp and often featuring as few as two rooms, set in a classic high-ceilinged townhouse, they are run by obliging owners who are quick to share their tips on the city. These excellent venues range in style, from the baroque Charles Rogier XI (Karel Rogierstraat 11, T 475 299 989) and bijou Thomas' Angels (Britselei 16, T 473 867 583) to the minimalist and tranquil Room National (opposite). For the full boutique-hotel experience and service to match, the best options are the Hotel Julien (see p022) and the spacious De Witte Lelie (Keizerstraat 16-18, T 03 226 1966).

Antwerp's hospitality scene clearly doesn't stay still for long and several new venues are to be completed over the next few years, including a sleek hostel in the Old City, designed by architects Vincent Van Duysen and due to open in late 2008; Mae, the city's first spa hotel; and the Qbic Hotel (Lange Koepoortstraat 2-4, T 043 321 1111), a contemporary, neon-lit venue that will house a brasserie run by the respected local restaurateur Vinko Pepa. *For full addresses and room rates, see Resources.*

Room National

Located across the road from ModeNatie (see p029), in the heart of Antwerp's fashion district, Room National was created by designers and sisters Violetta and Vera Pepa. Often hosting clients and creatives in their own home, they decided to create a B&B directly above their store on Nationalestraat (see p083). Working with local architect Jo Peeters, they opened this stylish venue in 2007. Room National is divided into one room, Erotic, and two suites, Zen (above) and Vintage, each with a different theme and décor, though all featuring clean lines and sleek furnishings. Future plans for the interiors include the addition of artworks chosen by the sisters. *Nationalestraat 24, T 03 226 0700, www.roomnational.com*

Het Luxepaard
This striking B&B housed in a grand
art nouveau residence is the brainchild
of artists Hubèrt van der Meer and Henk
Duijn. Choose between the Red Suite
(pictured) and Garden View Room, both
of which were decorated by the couple,
who are happy to advise guests on
Zurenborg's architectural treasures.
*Lamorinièrestraat 250, T 03 290 5641,
luxepaard.be*

Hotel 't Sandt

Situated within minutes of the Old City, the river and Sint-Annatunnel (see p014), across the street from Kloosterstraat's antiques market, this charming four-star hotel has a traditional interior and feel. Opened in 1993, the year Antwerp was nominated European Capital of Culture, 't Sandt is spread over four floors and includes 29 rooms, all styled by one of the owners, Ronald Lauwers; we recommend the Cathedral Penthouse (above), a Luxe Suite. The service here is top-notch and the hotel's business facilities include four large meeting rooms. There's also a small but pleasant terrace garden.
Zand 13-19, T 03 232 9390,
www.hotel-sandt.be

Miauw Suites

The concept here is simple and effective: well-sized suites kitted out with carefully selected contemporary furniture, located in the most fashionable part of town. Set in a corner building on Marnixplaats, Miauw has three accommodation options, one on each floor, offering large spaces in which to sleep, lounge and work. The open-plan ground floor currently houses a café and a variety of art and commercial projects, but owner and fashion designer Analik Brouwer plans to install a retail point for Miauw-branded products, from clothes and furniture to art, as well as another coffee bar. For the best views, reserve the third-floor Black Suite (above). *Marnixplaats 14, T 03 248 4707, www.miauw.com*

Hotel Julien

One of Antwerp's first boutique hotels, and occupying a 16th-century building, the Julien opened in 2004. Its interiors carefully balance period features, such as the finely crafted doors and ceilings in the breakfast hall and lobby (above), and minimalist contemporary design. The hotel's 11 rooms are divided between several levels and all overlook a tranquil central courtyard. As well as the top-floor Room With A View, the largest option, we recommend you reserve one of the Executive Rooms, whose characterful interiors are a little more rustic. The excellent, highly personalised service at Julien includes breakfast to order. *Korte Nieuwstraat 24, T 03 229 0600, www.hotel-julien.com*

Boulevard Leopold

It took nine months and a lot of hard work for Bert Verschueren and Vincent Defontaines to restore and decorate the 1890 house in which they opened this B&B in 2006. Boulevard Leopold comprises three rooms and two larger apartments, furnished with antique finds from the fleamarkets of Barcelona, the Dordogne and Antwerp. The owners' easy-going attitude and Leopold's relaxed atmosphere make guests feel instantly at home. Opt for the monochrome Room 1 (above); or if you want more space, Apartment 1, which includes a kitchen, two bedrooms and a bathroom with its original tiles.
Belgiëlei 135, T 486 675 838,
boulevard-leopold.be

24 HOURS
SEE THE BEST OF THE CITY IN JUST ONE DAY

In Antwerp, so many venues are within strolling distance that if one day is all you have, it'll be enough to get a sense of the city. Walking, especially in the centre, will give you time to admire the eclectic architecture of Zuid, and window-shop along the narrow streets of the historic centre and Meir. If you do want to use public transport, or head a little further out, Antwerp's efficient network of trams and buses and its metro system are all easy to navigate.

Any visit should include a tour of the Rubenshuis (Wapper 9-11, T 03 201 1555), the 17th-century Italianate villa partly designed by the artist, where he lived and worked. To discover the contemporary Belgian arts scene, head to MuHKA (overleaf) and ModeNatie (see p029), the focal point for the city's fashion community, which is located in a hotbed of high-end emporiums. If you have time, the FotoMuseum (Waalse Kaai 47, T 03 242 9300) and the Museum Plantin-Moretus (Vrijdagmarkt 22, T 03 221 1450), which specialises in the history of printing, are also worth a visit.

As for eating and drinking, Antwerp boasts a host of impressive restaurants and bars to satisfy even the most gastronomically demanding tourist. On your culinary tour, just make sure you try some *frites* – one of the best places to order this local speciality is the industrial-style Haute Frituur (see p028) – and Belgian waffles at Désiré de Lille (Schrijnwerkersstraat 16, T 03 233 6226).
For full addresses, see Resources.

10.00 Revista

A haunt of the creatives who work in the studios of trendy Zuid, this café opened in 2006. A hip spot at which to start your day, it offers teas, excellent coffee and a fine selection of pastries, as well as newspapers, design magazines and wi-fi internet access. Revista was conceived by its owner, Michiel Thys, who worked with the Brussels-based firm Pauwels-DeHaas Architecten to create an airy, streamlined, contemporary space. Grab a stool at the long counter next to the display of magazines and enjoy. The café counts painter Luc Tuymans among its regular customers, and if he likes it, so we. *Karel Rogierstraat 47, T 474 775 112*

11.00 MuHKA

Antwerp's Museum of Contemporary Art (MuHKA) has been promoting both Belgian and international art since 1987; Polish-born Goshka Macuga's *When Was Modernism* is pictured (left). The building, a former grain silo, dating from 1926, was designed by local architect Michel Grandsard, and includes later extensions into the adjoining warehouse; an entrance hall was added by Robbrecht en Daem in 2003. The exhibition space, around 4,000 sq m over six floors, displays MuHKA's permanent archive, which includes the Gordon Matta-Clark Foundation collection, as well as temporary shows. Take the lift to the third-floor café for excellent views of the city and to admire Belgian artist Hugo Duchateau's *The Ever Growing Ladder* installation inside the lift shaft. *Leuvenstraat 32, T 03 260 9999, muhka.be*

13.30 Haute Frituur

This recent addition to Antwerp's *frituur* scene, opened in September 2007, has quickly become a hot spot. Owner Michel Neubus previously ran two of the city's more intriguing interiors stores, which are now closed, and his idea for serving *frites* in a contemporary space proved spot on. He furnished it with Kartell furniture, and as if in response, Kartell opened a store down the road a few weeks later. Neubus has ambitious plans for at least 10 more Haute Frituurs. Order *frites* with tartare sauce, reckoned to be the city's best.
Vlaamsekaai 66

15.00 ModeNatie

An unmissable destination for fashion lovers, ModeNatie is a multilevelled platform for Belgium's fashion discourse, comprising the Flanders Fashion Institute (T 03 226 1447), MoMu fashion museum (T 03 470 2770), the editorial department of *A Magazine*, a library and the fashion department of Hogeschool Antwerpen (T 03 213 7100). The pizza-slice-shaped building that houses all these offices was renovated in 1997 by the Ghent-based architect Marie-José Van Hee, who created sleek, geometric, dark-wood interiors as a contrast to the classical cupola-topped exterior. ModeNatie is also home to the Copyright bookshop (see p084) and a Yohji Yamamoto store (T 03 213 2178). *Nationalestraat 28, modenatie.com*

20.00 Hippodroom

One of the hippest places to eat out in Antwerp is one of its most established restaurants, Hippodroom, which since 1999 has been satisfying local diners with its French-Belgian cuisine (try the lobster) and well-edited international wine list. Situated in an old townhouse, opposite KMSKA (see p009) and only steps from Ann Demeulemeester's store (see p086), the restaurant was designed by highly respected Belgian architect Jan Meersman. Featuring traditional brasserie materials – marble, velvet and brass – the interior is decorated with artworks by Belgian artist Michel François and tubular ceiling lights. The sheltered back garden is a lovely place to have lunch or dinner in summer, though our favourite spot is undoubtedly the brass-clad bar, where you can mingle with Antwerp's cool crowd.
Leopold De Waelplaats 10, T 03 248 5252, www.hippodroom.be

URBAN LIFE
CAFÉS, RESTAURANTS, BARS AND NIGHTCLUBS

Antwerp's laid-back, easy-going vibe is reflected in its nightlife. With the city's thriving fashion industry drawing a steady flow of style-conscious travellers to its eateries, bars and dancefloors, the city is enjoying a boom, and its reputation as a party destination is growing. For a town of this size, there's a high number of top-class restaurants to choose between, whether you're looking for a casual bar/bistro or a high-end dining salon. And the food you will be served – French, German, Italian, fusion, as well as local specialities such as Flemish stew and *frites* – is generally excellent.

The upscale and more traditional restaurants to try include Het Pomphuis (Siberiastraat z/n, T 03 770 8625) and Sir Anthony Van Dijck (see p042), while two of the best contemporary options are Hippodroom (see p030) and Hungry Henrietta (see p048). And don't leave town without having visited Dôme (see p040) and De Kleine Zavel (opposite). Local restaurateur Vinko Pepa specialises in stylish but informal eateries, which are ideal choices for a snack or coffee; Kapitein Zeppos (see p036) is one of the most popular.

The after-hours scene in Antwerp caters for all tastes. Head to Het Eilandje for dance clubs housed in industrial-style spaces, such as Noxx (see p052), the classic Café d'Anvers (Verversrui 15, T 03 226 3870), or bar-hop between Zuid's smaller, cosier boltholes to trend-spot and sip cocktails or sample Belgium's fine beers. *For full addresses, see Resources.*

De Kleine Zavel

This relaxed restaurant owes its decade of success to a combination of exceptional food, excellent service and its convivial atmosphere. Don't be fooled by the low-key bistro-style interior, designed by chef Carlo Didden in collaboration with local artists – De Kleine has been recommended in the *Michelin Guide*. The food is described as 'French fusion', and there's an emphasis on fish; we recommend one of the raw tuna preparations or roasted brill with tartare of crayfish and crustacean béarnaise. The ever-evolving wine list is praised by fashion designers Violetta and Vera Pepa (see p083), who are regulars. For an intimate supper, reserve table nine, tucked between the wooden crates that date from when the building was a hotel for the shipping industry. *Stoopstraat 2, T 03 231 9691*

Ferrier 30

When local architect Sofie Pittoors was asked to renovate Ferrier 30 in 2004, she created a sleek new space, setting black furnishings against white walls: the perfect backdrop for the restaurant's collection of contemporary photography and art. Co-owner and chef Stefano Lampis hand-picks high-quality ingredients, which he transforms into modern Italian cuisine; specialities of the house are *vittello tonnato*, a dish of very thinly sliced veal with a tuna and mayonnaise sauce, and the delicious *costata di manzo alla fiorentina*, using the best Belgian beef loin. Its first-rate food, stylish design and prominent position opposite KMSKA (see p009) ensure Ferrier 30 is always buzzing with local creatives, so book well in advance, especially at the weekend.
Leopold De Waelplaats 30, T 03 216 5062

Kapitein Zeppos

Set on a quiet corner on the edge of the shopping district, Kapitein Zeppos, launched in 1998, has earned its place in the hearts of Antwerpians. Its owner, Vinko Pepa, is well known for his venues across the city, which include restaurants, brasseries and even guerrilla eateries. Zeppos has a friendly atmosphere, and a traditional wood-and-tile interior, decorated with images from *Kapitein* *Zeppos*, the 1960s Belgian TV series. This is a great stop-off for an espresso break, a light lunch or an early-evening beer.
Vleminckveld 78, T 03 231 1789, vinko.be

Grand Café Horta

Located in the heart of the Meir, this café lends itself to people-watching, thanks to its huge glass windows. Light, airy and high-ceilinged, it owes its name and style to the great Belgian art nouveau architect Victor Horta, and specifically his Maison du Peuple in Brussels, which was razed in 1965; in fact, parts of the iron framework of Horta's masterpiece were used in this café's construction, which was designed by architect Willy Verstraete. Order from a menu that includes French, Flemish and Italian dishes, or just sup a Westmalle Tripel at the bar while you admire Café Horta's flowing staircase and ceiling. *Hopland 2, T 03 232 2815, www.grandcafehorta.be*

Hecker

There is no better way to finish off a day of antiques shopping on Kloosterstraat than dinner at Hecker. The restaurant's owner, Kasper Kurdahl, bought the space in 2002, and today this cosy, informal venue attracts architects, antiques dealers and fashion designers. A tempting list of delicate dishes is on offer, such as black duck with spring onions and asparagus, or yellowfin tuna with mesclun salad.

The long wine list features 130 bottles, including fine wines such as Opus 1 and Château Latour, and biodynamic bottles from Californian vineyard Bonny Doon.
Kloosterstraat 13, T 03 234 3834

De Biologisch-Dynamische Bakkerij

Chilean-born Carlos Maldonado has been doing business in Antwerp for more than 10 years, and this is his second branch of De Biologisch-Dynamische – the first is at Volkstraat 17 (T 03 216 0042). The concept is a bakery/café, where, as well as sampling delicious homemade breads and pastries, and indulging your sweet tooth on sugary treats, you can come for a light supper. Designed by Bellemans Cory and Maldonado himself, the space boasts attractive wooden floorboards, original patterned tiles and a hand-painted mural on one wall. In summer, you can sit on the terrace at the back.
Mechelsesteenweg 72, T 03 248 7800

Dôme and Dôme Sur Mer

This pair of sleek restaurants, opened by chef Julien Burlat, former Dries Van Noten stylist Sophie Verbeke and architect Paul Wauters, are two of Antwerp's finest eateries. The first, Dôme (above), housed in a late 19th-century building, formerly a teahouse, boasts an exquisite original mosaic floor and dome (registered as a city monument), and serves a French-influenced menu; it won a Michelin star in 2006. The second, Dôme Sur Mer (left), is a collaboration between Burlat and Verbeke and their friend Julien Bobichon. The décor here is contemporary and the focus is on seafood, hence the aquarium. For pastry-lovers, the same trio is behind the pâtisserie Domestic (T 03 239 9890). *Dôme, Grote Hondstraat 2, T 03 239 9003; Dôme Sur Mer, Arendstraat 1, T 03 281 7433, domeweb.be*

Sir Anthony Van Dijck

It's not easy to find Sir Anthony Van Dijck, but it's worth the search. Located in Vlaeykensgang, an historic alley off Groenplaats and Grote Markt, the 16th-century building was lovingly restored and decorated by local antiques dealer Axel Vervoordt, in a style similar to that of a middle-class townhouse at the time of Van Dijck. The elegant environment is matched by immaculate service and flawless food: French with a Belgian twist, with an accent on fish. The restaurant was twice awarded a Michelin star under chef/owner Marc Paesbrugghe. Reserve a table near the inner courtyard (above) for the views onto the garden.

Vlaeykensgang Oude Koornmarkt 16,
T 03 231 6170, siranthonyvandijck.be

Mogador

If antique-hunting in Sint-Andries or trawling the boutiques of Zuid has tired you out, take a breather at Mogador. This stylish bar is run by good-looking staff who mix a mean cocktail, notably a wonderful caipirinha. Minimalist black leather seating, low tables, chandeliers and white walls make up the contemporary interior. The space may be small, but the amicable atmosphere at Mogador makes it a pleasure to hang out in; in summer, the terrace, which overlooks KMSKA (see p009), is great for people-watching.
Graaf van Egmontstraat 57,
T 03 238 7160, mogador.be

Lux

The idea here was to create an all-in-one venue for a total evening's entertainment: cocktails and appetisers at the long bar, dinner in the restaurant, then after-hours partying in the vaulted basement lounge. Housed in a former Polish shipping company headquarters, Lux opened in 2003. It was designed by the owner in collaboration with Jeroen Verreydt, who added modern touches to the original features, which include marble columns, parquet flooring and an ornate staircase. Given Antwerp's maritime history and Lux's location in Het Eilandje, it comes as no surprise that a fish platter, with lobster, scallops, shrimps and mussels, is among the house specials on the French/Belgian/Italian menu. Ask for a table on the first floor, where you'll get the best views of the docks.
Adriaan Brouwerstraat 13,
T 03 233 3030, luxantwerp.com

Bitterpeeën

This family-owned, wood-and-mirror-clad eaterie, managed by Eddie Van Collie, has been up and running since 1994. Featuring traditional Belgian and French food, the menu includes robust dishes such as bone marrow, *carbonnades à la flamande* (Flemish veal stew cooked in black beer), ham with a mustard sauce and *bollekes van den Dam* (meatballs in tomato sauce, with celery and carrots). The live music most nights, slick service and cosy feel have made this off-the-beaten-track venue, located on the north-east fringes of Het Eilandje, a popular choice for the local art and business crowd.

Ijzerlaan 26, T 03 227 4696, bitterpeeen.be

Café Hopper

An institution on Antwerp's nightlife scene, this small, retro jazz café is always packed. Wooden 1950s-style chairs, tiles and a piano call to mind a Parisian *boîte*, which here comes with views over Zuid and a great location, just minutes away from some of the city's best restaurants and cultural venues. Open during the day, making it a good stop for a coffee or beer, Hopper comes into its own at night, when local and international jazz musicians attract Antwerp's musos and hipsters.
Leopold De Waelstraat 2,
T 03 248 4933, hopperjazz.org

Hungry Henrietta

One of only a handful of restaurants with a contemporary interior in Antwerp's historic centre, Hungry Henrietta moved to its present location in 1999, but has been run by the same family since 1973. The main dining space, set in a Bob Van Reeth-designed building, is a concrete-and-glass box with a glossy black finish and mirrors; the furniture includes pieces by the Eameses and Maarten van Severen.

Henrietta serves several dishes which, due to popular demand, have stayed on the menu for years, such as North Sea sole with grey shrimps and sour cream. Regulars include a number of local architects, like Vincent Van Duysen and B-architecten, and chef Olivier Cielen has also cooked for Belgian royalty. Everyone receives the same impeccable service. *Lombardenvest 19, T 03 232 2928*

Refectoire

What does a high-fashion manager do
when he wants a change of direction?
In John Dejans' case, he opens a restaurant
After leaving Ann Demeulemeester's store
(see p086), Dejans decided to follow his
childhood passion – cooking – by opening
Refectoire in 2004. The building he chose
was once a cheese shop, then a butcher's,
and it still retains much of its original
character. Furnished with items Dejans
handpicked at antiques markets, it offers
Mediterranean cuisine and a few Belgian
specialities; Dejans recommends the
pigeon and peas, or oxtail stew. The small,
1940s tiled entrance may be unassuming,
but Refectoire's menu and warm, intimate
atmosphere has made it a local favourite.
Kleine Markt 4-6, T 03 234 3428

Black Pearl

One of the biggest clubs in town, Black Pearl is located in a converted brick warehouse. Opened in summer 2007, it draws a refreshingly diverse crowd of party people, from pop stars to politicians. The creation of interior designer Moreen Cremers, of Mc2 Amsterdam, the space features flower-shaped wooden cut-outs on the walls, striking chandeliers and a mezzanine with low furniture overlooking the main floor. Kick back with a house cocktail (blackberries, Eristoff Black Vodka and a fresh lime sour mix), and chill out to the soulful soundtrack.
Braziliëstraat 12, T 03 232 2629, blackpearl.be

Verso Martini Bar

On the ground floor of the multi-brand clothes store Verso, but with its own entrance and opening hours, this bar is one of the most stylish spots in town for a mid-shopping-mission cocktail break or a preprandial martini. The interior, by designer Will Erens and creative team Pur Sang, would be a fitting set for a Bond film, with its white, croc-clad walls and Italian marble surfaces. Numerous chandeliers, mirrors and soft furnishings complete the luxe look. Perch at the bar or settle into one of the cushy leather seats. *Lange Gasthuisstraat 11, T 03 226 9292, www.martinibar.be*

Noxx

One of the most recent and ambitious additions to Antwerp's list of after-hours venues, Noxx opened in September 2007, and is one of the biggest clubs in the city. The futuristic space, which was conceived by Pur Sang, comprises four large rooms, each with a different ambience and style of music, from house and electro to 1970s, 1980s and Latin. There is also a champagne bar, a restaurant/bar Fusiaa, a make-up studio in the women's loo and a 360-degree LED screen in the Dark Room. It's open from Thursday to Saturday only, but Noxx's party events, music selection, sleek interiors and frequently ordered champagne jelly with strawberries attract everyone from fashionistas to local indie band Deus.
Straatsburgdok-Noordkaai 3,
T 03 295 5465, noxxantwerp.be

INSIDER'S GUIDE

KRISTOF GELDMEYER, ARCHITECT

Kristof Geldmeyer was born, raised and educated in Antwerp and has spent most of his professional life as an architect there. He has travelled extensively, from The Gambia to Sri Lanka, but has worked at trend-setting local firm Vincent Van Duysen since 1997.

In summer, Geldmeyer often heads to the outdoor terrace at Zuiderterras (see p062) for lunch, where he orders the *tomates et crevettes* with *frites* and mayonnaise and a *bolleke* (a brown Pilsner beer produced in Antwerp). Breakfast here is also the best way to begin a day shopping for antiques in nearby Kloosterstraat. Elsewhere in town, he recommends Pazzo (Oude Leeuwenrui 12, T 03 232 8682), for its impressive wine list and Italian-Japanese cuisine, and Hungry Henrietta (see p048) – and not just because the restaurant is directly across the street from his office. 'It's a striking architectural space – black and simple – and consistently serves really great, honest food,' says Geldmeyer.

The architect loves to walk along Cogels-Osylei to admire the art nouveau architecture, followed by dinner at either Dôme or Dôme Sur Mer (see p040), for a taste of chef Julien Burlat's superb cuisine. In the evening, he likes to call in to Café Hopper (see p047), for its jazz music and interesting crowd. For an alternative night out in summer, he'll get together with friends for a picnic on the north side of the river, to take in the great views of the city.

For full addresses, see Resources.

ARCHITOUR
A GUIDE TO ANTWERP'S ICONIC BUILDINGS

Much of Antwerp's architectural landscape reveals both the city's wealth throughout the centuries – as seen in its majestic Gothic landmarks, such as the Cathedral of Our Lady (see p011) and the Stadhuis (Grote Markt 1, T 03 220 8020) – and its inhabitants' great style and appreciation for the arts, as boasted by the neo-baroque Opera House (Frankrijklei 3, T 03 202 1011) and Zuid and Zurenborg's immaculate art nouveau and art deco townhouses, notably the magnificent residences on Cogels-Osylei.

For a tour of Antwerp's modernist gems, head south to the residential developments in the suburb of Het Kiel, Le Corbusier's Haus Guiette (see p066), the cultural complex deSingel (overleaf) and the Middelheim Museum Pavilion (see p068), designed by Antwerp's home-grown modernist Renaat Braem. For a snapshot of its contemporary architecture, beeline for Het Eilandje, whose regeneration was kickstarted by Robbrecht en Daem's Sint-Felix Pakhuis (see p070). A new City Museum, designed by Neutelings Riedijk, is due to open in 2009, while Diener & Diener, David Chipperfield and Gigon/Guyer all have projects planned.

Antwerp is the home of many of our favourite architects, such as Vincent Van Duysen and B-architecten, and the lively local design scene, promoted by the fledgling but very active Flemish Architecture Institute, promises an exciting future.

For full addresses, see Resources.

Van-Roosmalen-Haus

Designed partly in homage to Austrian architect Adolf Loos, and partly as a reminder of the city's maritime history, the Van-Roosmalen-Haus is a private residence, owned by designer and art collector Will Van Roosmalen – but it remains a not-to-be missed stop on any tour of Antwerp's architecture. The house was finished in 1985 and designed by Bob Van Reeth, its monochrome stripes referencing Loos's unrealised blueprint for singer and dancer Josephine Baker's home in Paris. It was the first piece of architecture that had been built facing the Scheldt in several years.

Sint-Michielskaai/Goede Hoopstraat

deSingel

Probably the best-known modernist building in Antwerp, deSingel is a cultural complex created as part of architect Léon Stynen's urban vision for the Wezenberg area. The total plan was never achieved, but construction on deSingel began in 1964 and was completed in stages until 1987. The interaction between the various tenants, which include the Royal Flemish Conservatory of Music, Belgium's Radio 2 and the Flemish Architecture Institute, is supported by the complex's shape, layout and concept: a combination of volumes of varying heights, bright corridors and airy halls overlooking an inner courtyard. An extension designed by Stéphane Beel is expected to be completed by 2010.
Desguinlei 25, T 03 248 2828, desingel.be

Renaat Braem Huis

There are many opportunities to admire Renaat Braem's work in Antwerp, including the Oudaan Police Tower (see p010), the Middelheim Museum Pavilion (see p068) and the Arenaplein mixed-use development in the suburb of Deurne. But a visit to the great Belgian modernist's own home, also in Deurne, is a must. Completed in the late 1950s, the exterior is a geometric play of brick volumes that creates large openings and an open-plan interior split across three levels; inside, Italian and Danish furniture is arranged functionally to serve both the house and Braem's studio. From the library to the living area, the interior is filled with original objects and pieces that illustrate the architect's lifestyle and express his modernist experimentations. Visits are by appointment only.
Menegemlei 23, T 03 314 5849

Zuiderterras

Winner of the prestigious Mies van der Rohe Award in 1992, Zuiderterras was designed by Bob Van Reeth and built between 1989 and 1991. Appearing like a ship moored on the Scheldt's right bank, its café and restaurant offer panoramic views of the city, and it's the ideal stop on an afternoon stroll along the Zuiderterras riverbank promenade. Van Reeth's design combines metal and glass to create a transparent, accessible building, whose form was based on the original 1886 Zuiderterras, a neoclassical building that burned down in 1973. Van Reeth's new structure features obvious references to Antwerp's maritime heritage, ranging from the small round windows to the cylindrical tower, and combines them with clean-lined, geometric shapes.
Ernest Van Dijckkaai 37, T 03 234 1275, www.zuiderterras.be

Designcenter De Winkelhaak

This simple, concrete-and-glass building, conceived by young architects Coby Manders and Filip Pittillion, was part of the regeneration of a rundown area around Centraal Station (see p009), and was opened in 2002 to provide a forum for up-and-coming design talent. Exhibition space, a shop, workshop areas, a library, a café, meeting rooms and office space are all enveloped within a double skin of glass and shutters made of perforated aluminium. Luc Vincent's interiors, visible from the outside when the shutters are open, feature a mix of materials – soft wood, Plexiglas, gold-lacquered metal – to produce a warm, inviting environment.
Lange Winkelhaakstraat 26, T 03 727 1030, www.winkelhaak.be

Haus Guiette

When he commissioned Le Corbusier to design his home in 1925, Antwerp-based painter René Guiette hoped to spawn a modernist community in the city. The house, including the artist's atelier, was finished in 1926 and is the city's only built work by the great modernist. An obvious Corbusier creation, it was designed as 'the perfect box': natural light pours in through generously sized windows, simple lines are used throughout, and the interior is shaped by an open-plan composition of planes and volumes. The front and back façades are mostly glass, while the sides have smaller windows, allowing the concrete walls to dominate. The house was restored and a studio added by architect George Baines in 1988. Sadly not open to the public, the house is the private residence of Ann Demeulemeester and her husband, Patrick Robyn.

Populierenlaan 32

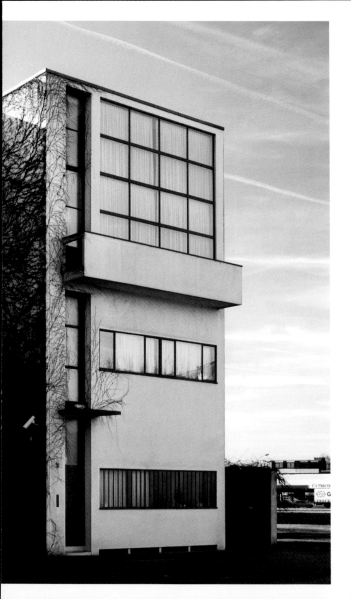

Middelheim Museum Pavilion

A former trainee of Le Corbusier, Renaat Braem was the architect responsible for the design of the main pavilion in the city's open-air Sculpture Museum Park. Tucked between trees and sculptures, by among others, Auguste Rodin and Dan Graham, the pavilion was opened in 1971 to protect some of the more vulnerable artworks from the elements; it also hosts temporary exhibitions. Braem's bright white, single-space design features one fully glazed wall and sculptural forms, including bird-shaped roof openings. Everything, from the door handles and furniture to the sleek black toilet basins, was designed by the architect.
Middelheimlaan 61, T 03 827 1534

Sint-Felix Pakhuis
This large 1859 warehouse, originally
designed by architect Felix Pauwels, is
now the home of the Felix Archives of the
City of Antwerp. The building was recently
given a tip-to-toe makeover by the Ghent-
based architects Robbrecht en Daem,
and reopened its doors in 2006. The
structure comprises two parts, divided
by the monumental covered main loading
area. The 24,430 sq m building has four
floors housing the archives, while the
ground floor includes public spaces, such
as the library; the refurbished top floor
has reading areas, meeting rooms and
conference halls. Wood is used extensively
throughout the interior, and the furniture
was also designed by Robbrecht en Daem.
Open to researchers only, the Sint-Felix
Pakhuis can be visited by joining one of
the regular tours of the building.
Oudeleeuwenrui 29, T 03 292 9411,
www.felixarchief.be

SHOPPING

THE BEST RETAIL THERAPY AND WHAT TO BUY

In the 1980s, the Antwerp Six – designers Walter Van Beirendonck, Dirk Bikkembergs, Ann Demeulemeester, Dries Van Noten, Dirk Van Saene and Marina Yee – put the city on the global fashion map. Today, the flagship stores of Demeulemeester (see p086), Van Noten (see p082) and Van Beirendonck (see p080) still present avant-garde creations in equally forward-looking retail spaces.

The group created an ideal environment in which successive designers could thrive. Further boutiques to investigate include Louis (Lombardenstraat 2, T 03 232 9872), one of the first shops to sell the designs of the Antwerp Six and also a stockist of Martin Margiela and Raf Simmons, Stephan Schneider (Reyndersstraat 53, T 03 226 2614), and several of the international brands here, such as Missoni (Frankrijklei 70, T 03 234 1778), whose store was designed by B-architecten. Lombardenstraat and Nationalestraat are the best shopping strips to check out emerging Belgian talent.

Even though Antwerp's retail scene is primarily associated with fashion, there are plenty of excellent product-design and furniture shops, such as Fiftie Fiftie (see p078) and Full Effect (Kloosterstraat 44a, T 04 8527 3282) for vintage 20th-century items; Donum (Hopland 47, T 03 231 3918) for contemporary pieces; and the antiques stores along Kloosterstraat. And make time to wander through Nieuwe Gaanderij, an elegant 1970s arcade.

For full addresses, see Resources.

Huis A Boon

Antwerp's style mavens pay at least one visit a year to Huis A Boon. The shop is small and unassuming, but it has been carrying an impressive range of high-quality leather gloves in a multitude of styles since it was established in 1884. Quirky but chic, the extensive selection includes lambskin gloves trimmed with rabbit fur, and wild-pigskin driving gloves lined with silk. Meticulously arranged in the drawers that line the walls, the gloves come in numerous shades and colours, from pinks and reds to browns and black. Huis A Boon also offers gloves and mittens in other materials, such as lace.
Lombardenvest 2-4, T 03 232 3387

FCS

Opened in late 2007, FCS, which stands for Furniture and Clothing Selection, has gained a reputation as an essential stop on the vintage furniture and fashion trail, thanks to owner Jean Jacques' discerning eye. In his large Zuid store, you may come across modernist furniture, such as lamps by Gio Ponti, retro pieces by the Antwerp Six, or a rare dress by Keith Haring, as well as jewellery and accessories. FCS is a superior vintage-shopping experience, not only for its inspiring collection but also for the sleek space in which it is displayed. *Timmerwerfstraat 8, T 03 294 3378, fcselection.be*

Goossens

When you walk along the picturesque, cobbled Korte Gasthuisstraat en route to the Cathedral of Our Lady (see p011) or the haute-couture parade Hopland, it's impossible not to notice the long queue outside the tiny Goossens bakery. It is said to be the oldest in Antwerp, established in the late 19th century, and its sweet delights attract both locals and visitors. Goossens sells buns, cookies, pastries and fruitcakes, but is famed for its raisin bread, which is piled high in the window; try the apple bread too, which is equally delicious. Take your place in the queue – it'll be worth the wait.
Korte Gasthuisstraat 31, T 03 226 0791

Veronique Branquinho

Working with B-architecten, Veronique Branquinho opened her Antwerp store in a former jeweller's in 2003. The interior was preserved in its original state as much as possible, as the concrete, modernist style fitted perfectly with Branquinho's aesthetic. The ground floor displays womenswear, while the men's collection is on the first floor, showcased around the atrium. The windows that look out onto Nationalestraat contain two large light boxes, displaying black-and-white photos of a forest in winter – the image used to illustrate the Branquinho brand. *Nationalestraat 73, T 03 233 6616, veroniquebranquinho.com*

Fiftie Fiftie

Specialising in original vintage pieces by designers such as Charles and Ray Eames, George Nelson and the Belgian Alfred Hendrickx, Fiftie Fiftie is Antwerp's premier destination for 20th-century furniture. Owner Bill Kuijpers' carefully edited selection includes furniture and decorative art, as well as specialist books on industrial design. Highlights have included a cabinet by Osvaldo Borsani and Lucio Fontana, a two-seater 'How High The Moon' sofa by Shiro Kuramata and a pair of Carlo Bugatti chairs. Kuijpers' design advice is spot on, as is this white-tiled, open-plan jewel of a store.
Kloosterstraat 156, T 495 150 775, fiftie-fiftie.be

Karin Nuñez de Fleurquin

Peru-born designer Karin Nuñez de Fleurquin has been making jewellery since 2003, and apart from creating her own lines, she has also collaborated with Walter Van Beirendonck, Bruno Pieters and Dries Van Noten. Nuñez de Fleurquin styled her Antwerp store herself, opting for black walls and display cases and cabinets. The clean and clutter-free style of the space complements the designer's strong, simple and occasionally quirky pieces, which include jewellery for women and children, and men to order.
Sint-Jorispoort 37, T 03 281 0474, karinnunezdefleurquin.com

Walter

Few shops in Antwerp are of such key importance to the international fashion scene as Walter Van Beirendonck's Walter. The store, a former car park, was conceived by the designer himself and B-architecten, who transformed it into a fitting space to showcase Van Beirendonck's pioneering fashion. The existing drive-in ramp and skylights were retained, the walls smoothed and painted white, and a polished-concrete floor added. Opened in 1998, Walter entered a new phase in 2006, adding lifestyle and furniture items. Some of the existing installations were removed and three bright yellow steel-frame structures were introduced. Walter also stocks designs by Jan & Carlos, Comme des Garçons and Bruno Pieters. *Sint-Antoniusstraat 12, T 03 213 2644, waltervanbeirendonck.com*

Dries Van Noten
Launched in 1989, this was Van Noten's
first shop and is located at one end
of Nationalestraat in the prestigious 19th-
century Het Modepaleis (Fashion Palace)
building, which was renovated by the
architects DMT. The men's, women's and
accessories collections are spread over
two floors, connected by a spiral staircase.
The classic white interior, with its wooden
fittings, Venetian-glass cabinets, marble,

parquet floors and luxe leather sofas and
chairs, forms a suitably stylish backdrop
for the designer's heavenly creations.
Nationalestraat 16, T 03 470 2510,
www.driesvannoten.be

Violetta & Vera Pepa

Sisters Violetta and Vera Pepa were born into a couturier family, and established their own Antwerp store in 2005. The duo's love of austere styles and clean lines is reflected in the interior, designed by architect Jo Peeters. The space is divided into an oak-parquet main retail area and the slightly darker and more intimate back hall (above). A Jean Prouvé table and two Gerrit Rietveld chairs are among the few pieces of furniture in the shop. In summer 2009, a clothing line will be added to the existing shoe collection. If you like the Pepas' style, their B&B, Room National (see p017), is located above the shop. *Nationalestraat 24, T 03 238 0021, www.pepa.be*

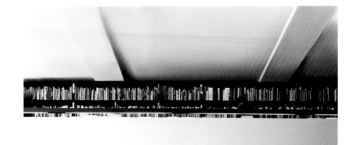

Copyright

When the Copyright bookshop moved
from its small premises in a narrow alley
to its current location in the ModeNatie
(see p029) building in 2000, it took
on a new character. The shop was designed
by architects Vincent Van Duysen to evoke
a combination of a library and a store,
stocking art, architecture and design titles
Echoing the classical architecture of the
ModeNatie building, the interior features
striking, dark marble floors, black and
white columns and beams, and dark-
wood-panelled bookcases.
Nationalestraat 28a, T 03 232 9416,
www.copyrightbookshop.be

Annemie Verbeke

B-architecten is the firm chosen by many Antwerp-based fashion designers, and Annemie Verbeke's shop demonstates why. The store, which is located on a corner, is fitted with mirrored walls in an art deco pattern that subtly enlarge the space, while black ceilings are offset against elaborate light fittings. The front area, naturally lit via two large glazed windows, is the showroom for Verbeke's collection, while behind this lies a more discreet area for trying on the designer's chic but playful clothes.
Nationalestraat 76-78, T 03 226 3560, annemieverbeke.be

Ann Demeulemeester

Designed in collaboration with architects Robbrecht en Daem, Demeulemeester's two-level Zuid store was conceived as an extension of her workshop. Featuring a monochrome scheme and an unpolished wood floor, this raw space, parts of which are wrapped in white linen, sells the designer's mens- and womenswear.
Leopold De Waelplaats/Verlastraat,
T 03 216 0133, anndemeulemeester.be

SPORTS AND SPAS

WORK OUT, CHILL OUT OR JUST WATCH

One of the best sporty activities to pursue in Antwerp is swimming, as the city boasts some fine pools. The open-air one in Boekenberg Park (see p094) is ideal for a splash in summer, while Olympisch Zwembad Wezenberg (overleaf) is the choice of serious amateurs and professionals. Another impressive indoor venue is the 1933 Veldstraat Pool (Veldstraat 83, T 03 259 2355), featuring original art deco windows and mosaics, which is slated to reopen after restoration by architect Rudi Mertens is completed in late 2008.

The city also has several stadiums and some good old-school gyms and fitness centres; often the most comprehensive facilities can be found in the city's modernist residential complexes – for example, the 1956 Renaat Braem-designed sports hall located in the Arenaplein development in the suburb of Deurne. In keeping with the relaxed nature of Antwerp's inhabitants, there's a good choice of spas too, such as the sleek Man Chi (see p092) or the more quirky Le Boudoir (Mechelsesteenweg 78, T 03 237 0835).

If you are looking to exercise outdoors or simply want some fresh air, spend a few hours in the city's best green space – the 130-hectare Provincial Park Rivierenhof (Turnhoutsebaan 246, T 03 360 5217), which has sports grounds and trails for numerous activities, such as cycling, jogging, football, tennis, pétanque and even fishing. Refreshments are served beside the small lake.
For full addresses, see Resources.

Bosuil Stadium

Architect Alfred Verdijck designed this stadium for his beloved Royal Antwerp Football Club in 1923, when its rising popularity meant the team and its fans had outgrown its previous home. Built to hold more than 38,000 spectators, the stadium was upgraded in the 1930s to hold 60,000. It began to deteriorate in the 1970s, but renovations in 1991 and 2001 returned Bosuil to its former glory.

This stadium and the Olympisch Stadion in Kiel, which hosted the 1920 Olympic Games, are the most important in the city. *Oude Bosuilbaan 54a, T 03 328 0860, rafc.be*

Olympisch Zwembad Wezenberg
The Wezenberg is the biggest and most
highly regarded of Antwerp's numerous
swimming pools. The main hall houses
the 50m-long Olympic-size pool, where
full-height windows look out onto the
woodland beyond. There is also a smaller
20m pool for children and beginners.
After a 22-month closure and extensive
refurbishment, the Olympisch Zwembad
today is an impressive facility with a
high-tech feel. And it is only a few steps
away from the deSingel arts complex
(see p058), making a combined sports
and culture outing possible. On occasion,
the pool is closed to the public for
swimming in order to host national
and international competitions, but
you can enter as a spectator to watch
galas and water polo matches.
Desguinlei 17-19, T 03 259 2311

Man Chi

Designed by Danny Venlet and owned by Anne Severyn, this urban retreat, spa and wellness centre, located in the heart of Antwerp, is tucked away on a quiet street. The therapies focus on Asian techniques, especially Chinese, Japanese and Thai practices, like pressure-point massages, facials and reflexology, and take place in a series of minimalist treatment rooms and massage 'pods'.

There is also a Turkish hammam. Try out a massage in the Man Chi chair, designed by Venlet and Severyn. Treatments use natural products, such as tea-tree oil, Moroccan argan oil and mud.
Ijzerenwaag 11, T 04 8668 4575, www.manchi.be

Boekenberg Pool

Antwerp's first eco-friendly open-air
pool, whose water is purified naturally
via its plantlife, is set in an attractive
park in Duerne that is also home to an
18th-century castle. The pool was closed
for some time while renovations were
carried out by German firm Dongus
Architekten, and was reopened in 2007.
It's open daily from July to September.
Van Baurscheitlaan, Boekenberg Park

ESCAPES

WHERE TO GO IF YOU WANT TO LEAVE TOWN

When it comes to travelling in Belgium, one of the country's biggest advantages is its compact size – at only 30,500 sq km, a trip abroad can be a daily experience for many of its citizens. Antwerp itself is just half an hour's drive from the Netherlands, and it's less than two hours by high-speed train to Germany or France. If you're feeling lazy, or simply want to be pampered, the B-architecten-designed travel agency Weekendesk (Kronenburgstraat 27, T 03 202 1660) can prepare an ideal getaway package for you.

Luxembourg (see p102), Liège and Maastricht (opposite) are ideal destinations for exploring the culinary and art highlights of the Benelux region. And if Antwerp's modernist architecture has whetted your appetite, head to Utrecht to visit Rietveld Schröder's house (Prins Hendriklaan 50) and Rotterdam (overleaf), to tour the wonderful Sonneveld House (Museum Park 25, T 00 31 10 440 1200), designed by Brinkman & Van der Vlugt in the early 1930s.

Closer to home, the affluent seaside resort of Knokke-Heist (see p100) in the north-east of Belgium is a draw for sun-worshippers, who rent holiday villas beside the pristine beach. And if, after appreciating Antwerp's docklands architecture, you are keen to explore the region's industrial hinterland, the Bauhaus-like former coal mine in Essen, Zeche Zollverein (Gelsenkirchener Straße 181, T 02 018 5430), would be a worthwhile half-day trip.

For full addresses, see Resources.

Maastricht, Holland

The boutique Kruisherenhotel (above; T 00 31 43 329 2020), housed in a converted 15th-century Gothic monastery, is an ideal base from which to explore Maastricht. The city has an enticing mix of fine restaurants, cultural venues and architectural highlights. Set against a backdrop of Romanesque churches, such as the Basiliek van Sint Servaas (T 00 31 43 321 2082) and Onze Lieve Vrouwbasiliek (T 00 31 43 325 1851) are a slew of stunning contemporary buildings, including the concrete-clad fire station (Prins Willem Alexanderweg), designed by Rotterdam-based architects Neutelings Riedijk, the 1993 extension to the Rijkshogeschool (T 00 31 43 346 6670), by Wiel Arets and Wim van der Bergh and the Bonnefantenmuseum (T 00 31 43 329 0190), with its striking zinc-clad dome designed by Aldo Rossi.

Rotterdam, Holland
Just over an hour's train journey from
Antwerp, Rotterdam has plenty of jewels
to offer the architourist, and is home
to many designers and architects, such
as MVRDV, Rem Koolhaas, Richard Hutten,
Joep van Lieshout and Wieki Somers.
The Museum Boijmans Van Beuningen
(right; T 00 31 10 441 9400) should
be your first stop, to view Robbrecht en
Daem's boxy 2003 glass-and-concrete
extension, works by the old masters and
the Netherlands' only surrealist collection.
Equally impressive is OMA's Kunsthal (T 00
31 10 440 0300). Not to be missed are the
Sonneveld House (see p096) and the Van
Nelle Factory (T 00 31 10 750 3500), both
designed by Brinkman & Van der Vlugt.
For panoramic views, scale the Euromast
tower (T 00 31 10 436 4811), and for dinner
book at Blits (T 00 31 10 241 1788), designed
by Mecanoo, with Marcel Wanders interiors.

Knokke-Heist

Located in north-east Belgium, Knokke-Heist is one of the country's best-known seaside resorts and a popular destination for Belgians, neighbouring Dutch and visitors from all over Europe. Blessed with white sands and featuring a wide promenade, it's also home to the country's most exclusive beach enclave, Knokke Het Zoute, the favourite haunt of the Belgian jet set. Here you can admire the large villas and follow in the footsteps of painters such as James Ensor, Alfred Verwee and Paul Delvaux by taking a stroll by the sea. Along the way, duck into Marie Siska (T 05 060 1764), the local tearoom famous for its signature clover-shaped waffles. The recipe dates from 1882, and has been ordered by celebrity guests from Josephine Baker to Ava Gardner.
knokke-heist.be

Luxembourg

Despite its small size, Luxembourg city has a considerable number of museums and cultural attractions; its old quarters and fortifications are a UNESCO World Heritage Site. The Philharmonie (above; T 00 35 226 0227), a poetic, elliptical building on place de l'Europe, designed by Paris-based architect Christian de Portzamparc, became an instant city landmark when it was completed in 2005.

Marvel at the 827 white steel columns that surround the building before joining a tour of the interior. Other gems on the Luxembourg trail include IM Pei's modern art museum Mudam (T 00 35 245 378 5960) and the Grand-Ducal Palace (T 00 35 247 962 709). If you visit the city in spring, you'll catch the Printemps music festival.

NOTES
SKETCHES AND MEMOS

RESOURCES
CITY GUIDE DIRECTORY

HOTELS
ADDRESSES AND ROOM RATES

Astrid Park Plaza 016
Room rates:
double, from €140
Koningin Astridplein 7
T 03 203 1234
parkplaza.com/antwerpbe

Boulevard Leopold 023
Room rates:
double, from €100;
Room 1, from €120;
Apartment 1, from €175
Belgiëlei 135
T 486 675 838
boulevard-leopold.be

Charles Rogier XI 016
Room rates:
double, €200
Karel Rogierstraat 11
T 475 299 989
charlesrogierxi.be

Hilton 016
Room rates:
double, from €200
Groenplaats
T 03 204 1212
www1.hilton.com

Hotel Julien 022
Room rates:
double, from €165;
Executive Room, €225;
Room With A View, €270
Korte Nieuwstraat 24
T 03 229 0600
www.hotel-julien.com

Kruisherenhotel 097
Room rates:
double, €315
Kruiserengang 19-23
Maastricht
T 00 31 43 329 2020
chateauhotels.nl

Het Luxepaard 018
Room rates:
Garden View Room, €80;
Red Suite, from €95
Lamorinièrestraat 250
T 03 290 5641
luxepaard.be

Miauw Suites 021
Room rates:
suite, €150
Marnixplaats 14
T 03 248 4707
www.miauw.com

Qbic Hotel 016
Room rates:
prices on request
Lange Koepoortstraat 2-4
T 043 321 1111
qbichotels.com

Room National 017
Room rates:
Erotic Room, €95;
Zen and Vintage Suites, €135
Nationalestraat 24
T 03 226 0700
www.roomnational.com

Thomas' Angels 016
Room rates:
double, from €125
Britse Lei 16
T 473 867 583
thomasangels.com
Hotel 't Sandt 020
Room rates:
double, €170;
Cathedral Penthouse, €300
Zand 13-19
T 03 232 9390
www.hotel-sandt.be
De Witte Lelie 016
Room rates:
double, from €295;
Presidential Suite, €525
Keizerstraat 16-18
T 03 226 1966
www.dewittelelie.be

WALLPAPER* CITY GUIDES

Editorial Director
Richard Cook

Art Director
Loran Stosskopf
Editor
Rachael Moloney
Author
Ellie Stathaki
Deputy Editor
Jeremy Case
Managing Editor
Jessica Diamond

Chief Designer
Daniel Shrimpton
Designer
Lara Collins

Map Illustrator
Russell Bell

Photography Editor
Emma Blau
Photography Assistant
Robin Key

Sub-Editors
Melanie Parr
Vicky McGinlay
Editorial Assistant
Ella Marshall

Interns
Nicky Ashwell
Karen Smith

Wallpaper* Group
Editor-in-Chief
Tony Chambers
Publishing Director
Gord Ray
Publisher
Neil Sumner

Contributors
Sara Henrichs
Pei-Ru Keh
Meirion Pritchard
Katrien Vandermarliere

Wallpaper* ® is a
registered trademark
of IPC Media Limited

All prices are correct at
time of going to press,
but are subject to change.

PHAIDON

Phaidon Press Limited
Regent's Wharf
All Saints Street
London N1 9PA

Phaidon Press Inc
180 Varick Street
New York, NY 10014

Phaidon® is a registered
trademark of Phaidon
Press Limited

www.phaidon.com

First published 2008
© 2008 IPC Media Limited

ISBN 978 0 7148 4893 8

A CIP Catalogue record for
this book is available from
the British Library.

Printed in China

PHOTOGRAPHERS

Kristien Daem
Sint-Felix Pakhuis,
pp070-071
Rotterdam, pp098-099

Mattieu Faliu
Luxembourg, pp102-103

**Sven Otte/
buchcover.com**
Knokke-Heist, pp100-101

Burkhard Schiltny
deSingel, pp058-059

Inge Vandamme
Antwerp city view,
inside front cover
Oudaan Police Tower, p010
Cathedral of Our
Lady, p011
Law Courts, pp012-013
Sint-Annatunnel, p014
KBC Tower, p015
Room National, p017
Het Luxepaard, pp018-019
Hotel 't Sandt, p020
Miauw Suites, p021
Hotel Julien, p022
Revista, p025
MuHKA, pp026-027
Haute Frituur, p028
ModeNatie, p029
Hippodroom, pp030-031
De Kleine Zavel, p033
Ferrier 30, pp034-035

Kapitein Zeppos, p036
Grand Café Horta, p037
Hecker, p038
De Biologisch-Dynamische
Bakkerij, p039
Dôme and Dôme Sur Mer,
p040, p041
Sir Anthony Van Dijck, p042
Mogador, p043
Bitterpeeën, p046
Café Hopper, p047
Hungry Henrietta, p048
Refectoire, p049
Black Pearl, p050
Verso Martini Bar, p051
Noxx, pp052-053
Kristof Geldmeyer, p055
Van-Roosmalen-Haus, p057
Renaat Braem Huis,
p060, p061
Zuiderterras, pp062-063
Designcenter De
Winkelhaak, pp064-065
Haus Guiette, pp066-067
Middelheim Museum
Pavilion, pp068-069
Huis A Boon, p073
FCS, p074, p075
Goossens, p076
Veronique Branquinho, p077
Fiftie Fiftie, p078
Karin Nuñez de
Fleurquin, p079
Walter, pp080-081
Dries Van Noten, p082
Violetta & Vera Pepa, p083
Copyright, p084
Annemie Verbeke, p085

Ann Demeulemeester,
pp086-087
Bosuil Stadium, p089
Olympisch Zwembad
Wezenberg, pp090-091
Man Chi, p092, p093
Boekenberg Pool, pp094-095

ANTWERP

A COLOUR-CODED GUIDE TO THE HOT 'HOODS

HET EILANDJE
The city's docks are transforming fast with warehouses converted into upmarket venues

OLD CITY
Come here for the historic monuments, cobbled streets, townhouses and quirky shops

MEIR
Grand rococo architecture dominates Antwerp's retail hub and commercial district

ZURENBORG
This 'hood boasts lovely squares, a villagey feel and art deco and art nouveau buildings

SINT-ANDRIES AND ZUID
Upmarket and hip, these areas brim with designer boutiques, antiques shops and galleries

DIAMOND DISTRICT
The centre of the trade since the 16th century is still packed with shoppers and jewellers

For a full description of each neighbourhood, see the Introduction.
Featured venues are colour-coded, according to the district in which they are located.